The poems in this collection are superbly responsive to immediate and subtle points of contact with the earth. Cannily aware of the double-edgedness of language—how it can reveal, evoke, but also overlay place and its history—this writer trusts the poetry, going where it leads, even or especially when it attends to small things, ones that seem unimportant. That's where it becomes a resonant instrument, one that vibrates with larger issues as and when it finds the wavelength. Read this collection as a whole and become an inhabitant of this one particular place and the world.

—Philip Gross, *Thirteenth Angel* (2022), *Between the Islands* (2020), *The Water Table* (2009), all from Bloodaxe.

In *Field as Auditorium*, we are invited to listen to the land as it speaks through the seasons. This collection of poems, elegant in their language and compelling in their forms, carves itself out of the intimate and expansive terrains of the natural world, uncovering the layers of history, human presence, and ecological transformation there. Over and over, the poems beckon us to observe, cherish, and revere the natural world and the truths it holds about our existence. This is a beautiful and moving collection.

—Chris Salerno, *The Man Grave* (Persea, 2021), *Sun & Urn* (University of Georgia Press, 2017)

Maura High is more than a field guide speaking of nature. In her poems—the songs, voices, and often unnoticed motions of nature, living and apparently unliving—are deftly represented and revealed. Here is earth at the roots: what might be hidden is revealed, plants that flower and vine are celebrated, and the work of burning and repairing are unified and understood. Enter this Auditorium to be entertained, educated, and more–immersed and delighted by High's astute engagements in her chosen fields.

—Paul Jones, *Something Wonderful* (2021), *Something Necessary* (2024), both from Redhawk.

Field as Auditorium

Maura High

REDHAWK
PUBLICATIONS

Field as Auditorium
Copyright © 2025 Maura High

ISBN: 979-8-89933-007-0 (Paperback)
Library of Congress Control Number: 2025946499

Cover Design: Erin Mann
Book Design: Erin Mann

Front cover art credit: Nerys Levy, *Dairyland Road Triptych*, mixed-media watercolor and water-soluble pen on paper, 9" x 36", 2014
www.nerys.levy.com, @neryslevy
Printed in the United States of America.

First printing edition 2025

Redhawk Publications
The Catawba Valley Community College Press
2550 Hwy 70 SE
Hickory NC 28602
https://redhawkpublications

CONTENTS

Here is the place; here the way unfolds.

—Dogen Zenji

The earth says have a place, be what that place
requires; hear the sound the birds imply
and see as deep as ridges go behind
each other.

—William Stafford

Land

It opens, and then opens again,
grows over, and changes,

lose-some, gain-some.

There were trees,
once, deer cover, and browse,

hunting grounds of hawk and owl, squirrel runs,

old stumps and bark, nothing
if not hospitable.

It was open:

to the chatter and shriek
of birds, to the occasional hunter

and bands of travelers, it was theirs.

Before surveyors and deeds, the rasp
of saws and bangs and clanks of wood

against wood, and iron

against iron. Hard
work, and sharp voices,

to the trees

that now were eyed
as so many board feet and fenceposts,

this one for the house, that for the barn, the rest,

firewood: open, always,
to what we need from it,

and what we bring.

It opened to pond and pasture,
to its fescues and grasses, the ditsy
calico of meadow flowers.

To dogs, now, and children, and bicycles,
ball-players, runners, under the eyes of the gone

trees and the ghosts of the first nations.

Stitchwork

Here's greenbrier
     trailing

from branch to twig:
green thorn,
     green stem,
          green leaves rising

alternate—taking turns

in sunflash and glow,

and like palms, reading
     the sky and being read;

at each leaf joint, a little
        stem jog to the left,
     a little stem jog to the right;

green line binding
self to self,
and you can follow it
     down hunters' trails and
tales,
     through pocosin,

     thickets of bay, briar, wax myrtle,
     bitter gallberry,
        to the houses

and outhouses and trailers
     strung along the roads,
     the thin grass, the curtained windows

13

Monoliths

These large rocks

that lie or stand athwart
our suburban lots—

what do we make of them?

Stone forts, childhood's pinnacles, portals
through which at any time we may step,

and all around us hear

the roar of wind, ice crackling, rain
sluicing down the crags and gullies of the ancient
                                    mountains,

at whose feet we scrape up a handful of wild soil,

all that remains of them and resists
our efforts at domestication.

Bolin Creek the Names

Creek:
as in *crick, crooked,*
not yet *river,*
wordings for us from your elsewhere, northlands,
windings across
your late-come, man's-land boundaries

> [these (words) for
> what gives you, or stalls you, what
> delights
> catches your eye, eyeing our
>
> branch and confluence
> meanders, kinks, braids, oxbows
> millraces
> abandoned
>
> a channel for stormwater
> the place of recreation, re-
> creation, re-invention: we are],

before all others,
in Tutelo-Saponi, the language finding itself again,
> *hewa*
> *okitgenkai*
> *mani*
> *mony shap*
> *nistek*
> *ne*
> *ne*
> *ne*
> *yamuyimen*

[speak forked water shallow
rock this here now sing],

on a map, we're blue lightning,
in water, the bang-bump and angling
of rock crumble, pollens, sand slurry, leaf speckle, scat,
splinters of wood and bone

[reflection, refraction,
leaf-branch, particolored sky
shattering, fractal],

and in your eyes, looking
down, through the fly-lens of water
to the corrugated bedrock—

Say whose stake and homestead, whose ground,
whose elders
coming to meet you here now

in Tutelo-Saponi,
hewa okitgenkai mani mony shap nistek
ne
ne
ne
yamuyimen

The Field Index
  —Abandoned field, Orange County, North Carolina

Asters: lesser stars in these constellations, for the native
bees, late-summer smatterings of a color I might call blue,
blue petals and fireworks along the margins of the track,
and

broomsedge, bluestems: stooped in the fall and
shimmering, shivering in the wind, spinning out seed, bird
fodder, tangled (insert here) into brambles, blackberries,
this year's, last year's canes knotting and weaving, and

crabgrass: crabby claw and crab leg of a herb: edges into
the wilding mint and onion grass, the tall stands of raggedy,
wing-stemmed (my favorite) crownbeard gone to seed,
where I am with my small dog, and

dogwood: not here yet, but it will come; also *redbud* (q.v.)
and holly; the birds will bring it, in their guts, its white
bracts and inconspicuous flowers, its small understory
leaves will open and turn into the sunlight, before the
canopy leafs out and shades

exotics: migrants, stowaways and hitchhikers, too much at
home; see *invasives*, stiff-stemmed privet with its small
dark leaves, and the clustered graceful arcs of autumn
olive, honeysuckle vines, dead *stiltgrass* flopped into heaps,
good for nothing except time

ferns: rise and unfurl like our letter *f*, old as fossils, here
before letters and fiddles and bows and Michaux and his
acrostics, first and last green under the trees, with

ghost plants: the ancestors, clusters rising from damp,

17

unsunned patches of leaves along the margins of wood;
also: smatterings of green-and-gold, the droop-headed
goldenrod

honeysuckle: announcing itself in scent on the wind and
winding up and around the living and the dead: colors coral
(see *natives*), creamy white curling to yellow (see *exotics*)

invasives, see exotics; index of vexed and vicious cycles;
see also, *kill*

jaywalkers: I, alive, among others, on and off the old farm
road, on pirate paths, seed-spreader, compacting soil,
alarming insects and deer, stealing berries and sprigs and
twigs and clumps of lichen or moss, colored leaves, I

kill: by ice and drought, sapsuckers, larvae, blight,
competition, succession (it happens, why do I grieve?),
deer rub and browse, humans; see *jaywalkers*

loblolly pine: its spiny cones and bundles of three long
needles green, or fallen and draped in the shrubberies; aka
oldfield pine, straight up, above all, old-meadow native
homesteader in the lobby-lolly soil of this wide floodplain

milkweed: var. swamp milkweed, its pink inflorescence
and faint scent, drawing monarchs among butterflies and
pollinators, queen of weeds, fecund, its large brittle-dry
pods burst and spewing cloudy seed over the bewilding
meadow

natives: as in, before our time here, before this language
and its metaphors and usages, before people, and which
we watch with sorrow as they fall back and dwindle, are cut
down; see *exotics*, see

oaks, passim, and Osage orange, spiny along the branch
bank, its large green nobble-skinned fruit fallen in the path
and long grass, bitter, slow to blacken and rot, unscavenged
by all but small seed-eaters

persimmon (native), privet (not; see *exotics*): one,
provender for all comers, all creatures, i.e., small bell-
shaped flowers, small sweet ripe fruits; the other just
minding its own business, i.e., to thrive

Queen Anne's lace: umbels and fine-cut leaves, branching
stems, aka wild carrot and medicine, queen unknown and
from elsewhere, and the lace medallions for her bodice and
gown, for her headdress, her cuff, all scattered to the people
(winged and crawling insects), self-seeding

red cedar: modest, upright, native, pioneer in this process of
succession, spindle of evergreen and scent rolled between
the fingers (here I am again, breaking the rule of no taking
and leaving of souvenirs); and redbud: see *understory*,
flights of pink-purple blossom in the spring woods,
pleiades, announcing light and wings again, after all that

stiltgrass: Japanese, *Microstegium vimineum*, in summer
blithe, feathery and green under the trees over creeper and
grass, but poor food, tick haven (see *exotics*; see also
jaywalkers); and sweetgum: all over this old field, native
and opportunistic, prolific and prodigal, *Liquidambar* of the
spiny round seedhead and star-shaped, lobed leaves, their
margins calling to mind (my mind) calligraphy or the
gestures of dance, delight of form that is mutable and has
prickly edges, deliquescence, decadence, a nuisance, really

tulip tree: *tulipifera*, the saplings standing here and there,
innocuous, like any other small tree, but give them time,

they'll rise; the yellow-and-pale green petals of their
flowers say in English "tulip," the Tutelo-Saponi name lost,
yellow-green the heartwood, yellow the leaves in fall, and
early to fall

understory: native holly and redbud and dogwood,
parsimonious and irregular in habit, sparse fruit, sparse
flower; now also autumn olive, privet, and exotic forbs and
 grasses, the introduced and naturalized, myself and dog
under the canopy

vines: Virginia creeper, close-to-ground native; grape vine,
gangly fox grape, looping and loping up branch and stem,
dbh often equal to small trees; poison ivy, not the
inconspicuous three-leaved forb of the northlands, but
(learn this, human) rampant, thick-stemmed, hairy vine,
stuck fast to the trunks of trees

winged elm: small tree of delicate, dry stem, and long,
corky flanges along its branches; old (to my eye) before it's
old, strange (to my eye); unknowable why those wings

x: *Xanthium* through *Xyris* in Radford's *Manual*, as in
chicory and the yellow-eyed grass; also, a sign for
canceling and for marking you are here, this is the place,
this, my mark, my thumbprint

yellow poplar: see *tulip tree* and weep

zigzag: of silk in the web of the orb-weaving spider,
homespun look-at-me and distraction, quirk among
zoologies of abandoned gardens and meadows; zee, zed,
the end of bee flights and alphabets

Erythronium americanum

To keep it, to see it, see it better, as it is

solitary small flower, yellow, on a thin stalk
six glossy petals curving back,
stamens dangling like the clapper of a bell

to give it to a friend, to anyone, to let it speak

for itself and its mottled leaf with the long rib
and curled rim, for the dabs of new green
and fern, splotches of white, its bedstraw

to feel its name in your mouth

trout lily, fawn lily, dog-tooth violet

the south wind knocking it about
how it rings to the east, to the west, to the north
how it opens as the day brightens, and before dusk
closes in on itself, nods itself to sleep
to write the requiescat before it vanishes

Embroidered Field

Who pulled the floss from the skein
and knotted it, choosing

among the colors of flowers the colors of these

perfect, impossible asters, flower within flower,
corymbs and umbels, stitched in a time, I will,

I will not, I will, I will not. Knot.

Who paused, who chose to be quiet
in the light of a window, whose skillful,

versatile hand laid it in an upstairs room.

Who tore it, who tried to mend.
Who took the cloth from the ragbag, who

wiped the oily crankshaft, the axle, and then his hand,

adding to these decorous flowers
his own scumble and patch.

Who found in the abandoned barn

a crumple, stiff with grease and dust,
which unfolded into a runner embroidered with flowers,

field that was and never was.

Promised Land
　　　　—For Nannie and Mary Blackwood

Two sisters, now dead,
looked out over this hayfield,

remembering the old road
between Chapel Hill and Hillsborough
and who knows what else

of girlhood and seasons,
the smell of men coming in from field,
woodlot, and byre,

their own sweat and dried
blood, tubs of clothes
soaking in soapy water.

What should be said and not said.

Jim Crow ended, debts were paid.
There were wars.
They, too, ended, and the men

who went, most of them, came back,
more or less whole.

In New Hope, North Carolina, hope
rose up and was erased
and raised again, reiterated,

hope, no hope, new hope,
in a name, a hymn, a clutch
of warm eggs in the coop,

corn kernels in a white enamel bowl.

A Creek, Too Small
      —Blackwood Farm, New Hope

to be named, begins seeping
under leaf litter and over rock sills,
circumnavigating roots and boulders;

the creek, making a way
for itself, first a clear channel,
then a swamp staked out

by beavers—among tussocks
of swamp grass and fern, sharpened
stumps, felled saplings,
small trees chiseled to heartwood;

whose name should be as long
as the water flowing in it

and as particular as the sounds
made by those who crossed
or skirted it, the scythes
and clanging buckets, the suck
and exhale of boots treading mud;

people should weep

when they hear it uttered, because
it speaks of griefs and forced labor
and the many, now dead, who drew water here

so it entered their bodies
and ran in their blood like stories

In These Woods

lichen is patient
crust and scale, bright
against the wet rock

rust and ochre, green-gray

Lichen as in, licks, nibbles into
these old lavas and tuffs—igneous
even they

give way, pit and splinter

wash down
into the decomposing leaves and husks
of seeds and cracked nutshells

Mouse, rabbit, squirrel, deer
cats domestic and feral, coyote
hawk, owl, crow, wren

find sustenance enough

as the trees find
roothold enough, among the stones
and boulders

The forest
the sticks and twigs
in the crook of my arm

and I, eye and ear
are the Earth's skin
and muscled body

leaf jig and rattlebone

Before This, the Occaneechi

> *Yīma ya–tī–pu–yuke–wa nēi,* You have lived here.
> —Corey Roberts, "A Grammar Sketch of
> Tutelo-Saponi"

Sunlight falls, as it always has
    betwixt, tremulous, slant
through the oaks, through the hickories
    story and understory
splatters over the rocks, the fallen leaves
    deer rut and ripening
and falls too as it never did
    in the buzz-cut, clear-cut
on the scarred hardtop, on cars
    revved-up present, in this time
capped meters, water mains
    power and light humming in the wires
on shingles and siding, fence posts
    colonized by mold and beetles

concrete and gravel driveways
    plantain and grass and creeper
the street quiet and orderly
    the old trails running below ours
waiting for dusk and the deer
    cross-creek and ridge-line
to step out warily and cross
    not one but a web of roads
from one yard to another, and fall
    corn patch, paw-paw, muscadine
to grazing, for the old hunters
    the songs, the stamping feet
who wait in the shadows
    old words resurrected and invented

Excursions in Moss
        —for Barbara

They were here, all this time,
in this same world,
here for the seeing:

green shag and starfield, clumps, pinheads,
frilled with lichen,

and poking up through them the green
first leaves of violet, wood sorrel,
for example, among the ephemera—

here, in the piedmont of North Carolina,
all the greens in creation:

a landscape within landscapes,
slow as,
quiet as,

as back along
the rims of lakes and drainages in the early Cambrian.

In this same, old world:
the same creep and cling
and drill into the surface

with their fragile rhizoids, into rock fissures,
now bark, now exposed root,

into the Anthropocene and still
green between paving stones,
on verges, stuck fast

to rocks along the banks of Bolin Creek,
down a grit-and-gravel driveway.

A green gift
my friend gave me:
moss scrapings, from her yard

over in the next county;
in late summer

the waggly spore capsules
pop open, and a million spores float
off and up into whatever wind.

The Puddle

In a rut in the dirt road:
a vernal pool:
a few small,

almost transparent water striders
twitch the surface,
and below them,

tadpoles wriggle and float
in the limpid water,
hundreds of them—all

straining cell by cell to be
among the living,
the fat, full-throated racket

and splurge of spring
up and down the creek.

Pollen Counts

Here it comes, in great gusts off the loblollies, I see it! Fly up
and sift down, downdrift, spendthrift, anemophilous,
blind, how it loves the wind.

Heterodox, indiscriminate, miscellaneous—all the pollens at
once, grass and tree. The other fall. Into crannies and
puddles, marbling the glossy surface of water, a pale sheen
on window glass, on cars organza veils of dust, pollen on all
the leaves, on the barren ground of my old body, by the
wayside.

The long stringy oak catkins and the fat little caterpillar
stroboli of the pines, green turning brown, yellow turning
brown, and shriveling or sodden with rain on the back deck,
the stone steps and patio, among the creeping periwinkle of
the front yard, piling up at the sewer pipe across the creek, a
dam of scum and catkins.

Where does the body begin and end—in the wind, in the
micelium in the soil, among roots, and in the wooden bowl
on my desk, my desk?

And it wouldn't matter that you were half or more blind,
you'd know it was here, in your eyes in your nose in your
throat, as if you were some tree or early summer grass, some
discreet flower ready to be showered with gold, you could
feel it, gritty, powdery on glass, you could write *pollen* with
your fingertip in your best cursive on the car windows.

Passing

When was the tree no longer tree
and good for nothing
but kindling or compost?

Cell by cell by cell things happened
in the roots
in the twigs in the bark
come ice come air come deer in rut
fork and poison.

There was tree, green and flowing, then
lignum, carbon unmaking itself
atom by atom in the hot spring wind,
not so much
a becoming as a rising of something
brittle and eloquent, that was always there
like the red of leaves under green.

One kind of season has ended.
Stem and rootball with the clay
still clinging to it,
the hours
spent choosing and planting,
all the weeds ever pulled and tossed,
blackened slivers of wood, shreds of leaves—
into the wheelbarrow with all of them.

We Woods
> —Dry-mesic oak-hickory forest on a ridge along
> the north bank of Bolin Creek, central Orange
> County, North Carolina

Yes be a color—*nos & maybes,*
like drab.

Shrug, like slough-off,
peel, mould & mildew,
winterkill,

sometimes we surprise ourself
& sprout.

Tell ourself, this stem this leaf, vine,
oak, spindle, sucker, upstart hickory—

spring! we lagging over the redbud
(pink the redbud
& green leaf-leaf

dogwood), &
troublemaker
honeysuckle: they pull-us-down vines
pale, rampant.

Yes, we someplaces sick, crack, split,
stump & burl, rootballs what

gave up hanging in, dragged themself out & fell
up.

We woods, anyways: our down-
leaf & needlefall,
seedhoard, twiggery, sprig windfall,

they good, the earth approve,
let us rootway through dirt & stone.

Englynion for Fireflies

A rock, a flounce of leaves, flare in the sun.
A gleam of lichen.
A brief illumination

of green and rust, in the darkening wood.
A bright chord sounding
for a moment, and fading

back behind the old hickories and oaks.
Which then vanishes,
leaving dusk to the fireflies,

that rise now as if summoned and drift—down
there, up here, their soft
lights like voices on and off

and erratic above the damp, dead leaves
littering the wood.
Voices calling without words:

one another—not us—yet we light up
with them, and the night
frog calls, cicada, cricket.

Old Couple

If we had no human language
like those two red oaks outside the kitchen window
so close to each other among the rocks

each not an I but part we, root into root, branch
click and tick, crack

our leaves would be leafsmacking
our shshsh make-way make-space
negotiations

and the old dog's ashes washed down into our leafmould
our half-rotted twigs

the downed branch
its frills and flounces of jelly fungus, its crackling of lichen
would be our comforters

Creek Tell
　　　　—Bolin Creek, Orange County

We lap-lap & splash
up over & around the stones,
a chuckle, a hush,

settle, skim
off the dead leaf, the insect,
the pollen-&-crumb plant scum,

we come from up-
land, not far, there &
here, through dirt & root & leaves

running down, down,
we, as in made-of, as in
been-through

soil, dust & sand, shreds, shed
twig & bark,
lost seeds, root, flakes of vine,
& not done yet!,
hear these our long tongues,
our body,

scat & unnumbered
dead insect wing-
moult, cast-offs,

your here-today
stepping stones slurred, sliding
in our flood,

we know
braid, pool, splash & scrape, eddy,
do you hear the weight

we carry all the long down?
down, being creek being
water?

Verbesina occidentalis

Dark does not fall: it rises from the soil,
seeping along the flattened grass
of the dim path and flowing
up trees already black,
night's conduits, forked
darkening against the retreating light,
while below them in the field the crownbeard
on its winged stem makes a last effort,
waggling its two or three
yellow rays, lifting
its small cluster of disc petals
in imitation of the sun—though
its leaves have gone quiet already,
and the pollinators sleep their insect sleep.

*

Sleep is just a way to talk about what happens
in the dark, what cells do, what
color green is when no light shines on it
and nothing moves under the streetlights
in the ramifying subdivisions.
Wings close, and petals. Eyes
see nothing that is not inward and radical.
There are boundaries, such as where stem
becomes root, and where taproots probe
among stones, and we may travel them,
through capillaries and waterways and geographies
of decomposition. Underground
is a reflection of sorts, uncertain
and hopeful as seedheads at seedtime.

*

Seedtime is the wind, and seeds
quiver in their bracts, as brittle
as moths are, and as dry, as poised,
as these winged stems, which still lean
to the light. One good shake
and they scatter down the grasses
and lodge: while the rains come, and long hours
of dark and cold, while they parse
moonlight and sunlight, and know already
that the root comes first and follows water
down the kingdoms of soil, then a tendril
and the precursors of leaves, leaf, branch and crown.
I hold some in my palm: each husk ribbed and shaped
like a vase, like the word promise in their language.

*

In their language, *grow* is a conversation among cells,
why, because, you go first, yes you,
I this way and in this green vein
upward, here's sap sweet and mineral . . .
Like banners held to our view
by attending angels, their pronouncements
unfurl and flutter through the sunlight,
and all night they hum. The point being seed
and more seed, up where their lures dangle;
a few long, bright petals, no need
for more when bees enough roam the flowerets,
when even one person has leaned closer, as if to listen
and instead been sounded, like a drum
struck and reverberating through the field and further.

*

And further, along trails mapping
the wood, waysides—how many lives
did I pass through and never know its name?
By hearsay and looking, in a book, I found
a paradise of leaves, opposite and ovate,
that curious "tissue decurrent on the stem,"
the loose corymbs, taxonomies of desire
in a right name, a promise
of knowledge and belonging, as in "my flower,"
"my field," and so on, until "our flower,"
our dominion. That much was in my gift—a sprig,
it's true. While the flowers, which know all about
belonging, heeded light and wind,
water calling to them: *Verbesina*, little word.

*

Word, made dicotyledon and vascular,
one-stemmed perennial aster, of the family
Asteraceae: not so much star as constellation,
a coming-together years in the making,
from the time before the field, when it was still
wood down to the creek, before the field
was abandoned and grew over. Birds
fidgeted in the stands, deer
crashed through the stiff ribbed stems
and found shelter, people
walked with their dogs, Linnaeus
and his descendants were among the familiars.
We left traces on the leaves, on the grass
and track, a faint phosphorescence in the dark.

Englynion for Moss

Here's a canticle for mosses, plainsung,
brief notes, in minor keys—
for plants this small: small verses.

Moss-fur and moss-star, green skin and feathers.
No scent, nothing grand.
No dazzle, no flash, no sound.

No roots, no stems, no flowers, no seed,
no sap, no nectar.
In moss, nothing's vascular.

Water rising between the sporophytes
flowing up, a green rain
seeping through a green garden.

All those frills, spikes, spirals, fronds, threads, whorls spill
down the ragged columns
of the mind's herbarium.

Butterfly

A skipper,
immobile,
gold, amber, bark-brown,
sun and flame.

In a stand of crownbeard,
under the drooping nub of a flowerbud.

Little traveler,
Lon zabulon, Zebulun,

your names in our language
came from far and carry you further

than this old field and this season.

How far will you ride? How long
into the lives of my children
and their children?

Dog Days

The heat, the heavy
air make for a quiet
season.

Mushrooms

unfurl their pale,
thick flutes

at the base of an old maple,
each one cupping
a scant measure

of rain water.

Along the creek bed,
the diminished stream

slides over rocks
and gathers into pools.
Water striders dimple

the placid surface,

and twitch,
and from those centers spread
ring after ring,

reaching to the bank,
dislodging a particle
or two of clay—

and the earth
slides toward the equinox.

No Apples

But for those frosts, the crabapple
would be gravid with fruit now,

and the path beneath it
cobbled with June drops.

There would be a feast here
at the edge of the road,

not some green tree
bowed over the earth,

trying to draw from it
the old, faint smell of cider,

a memory of wasps
and mildew, bitter-sweet.

Reprise
> —for Frances

One leaf falls from the hickory
       outside my window—

       a slow loop right,
an about turn, and squiggle—

so cursory a gesture, it looks
       like something written

       in an alphabet of leaves:
a charm against insects

and woodpeckers; a plea
       for all the leaves that fall,

       blacken, and rot, and leach
into the earth, and rise again

to new petiole, new leaf,
       singing the green song of desire

       and the brown of thrift;
the whispery, creaky name

the tree gives itself;
       or the name we have given it,

       full of ourselves and our own
histories, as a child

writes her given name and sees
       herself there, her first self-portrait.

Dryocopus pileatus

Chek-chek, a red-capped woodpecker
        flew across my one good eye,
left to right and down, chek,
                and settled.

Dead poplar, maybe dead oak.

The same old native woodpecker
        that made one flute after another
        to give away, to console
like the wren and the warbler.

It takes practice and improvisation:
        chip and chisel, knock wood,
        its long beak prying
off, up, under, the sloughing, corrugated bark.

I am no predator, all ears I am, head cocked, listening.

Come on in. There's larvae,
        wintering beetles, there's
hide-and-seeking
        wood music, ready or not.

From the Fire Weather Observer's Log

Late November
        Wind 20ft/early (mph)   lgt/var
        Wind 20ft/late (mph)   lgt/var
        Vent Rate (mph-ft)   28500
        Burn Category   1

There's no good wind
there's wind that's good for

there's wind in the wiregrass
in the aerials

there are dry beech leaves at my feet
and more marcescent

on the trees dangling at the twig ends
as if shielding those spikes

that aren't thorns but tightly furled
tender leaf buds and

what wind will carry off the leaves
would take a storm and still

some would stick fast
petiole to twig they know

habits of the growing season
the past summer turned amber

turned copper-alloy parch-throat
choke and scratch

I'd wish to be as useful being dead
and as crackly

*

Mid-December
        Chance Precip (%)   90
        RH % (24h trend)   86
        Wind 20ft/early (mph)   S 10 G21
        Wind 20ft/late (mph)   S 12 G21

Probability of ignition zero
immaterial the wind

in the unit that burned yesterday
noone watches

the top-killed scrub-oak saplings
torch into no flames

noone's hand feels
along the charred logs

for no heat the sloughed bark
the ground sodden streaked with ash

the observer by habit now
notes down the wind rain fire

of the future Earth reads the leaves drab
reads limp the wet and dry bulb

thermometer of tree and twig
dormant dead dying dormant

*

Early February
        Chance Precip (%)   0
        RH % (24h trend)   45
        Wind 20ft/early(mph)   SW lgt/var
        Wind 20ft/late(mph)   SE 7

List of things to be included
belt weather kit soot-stained battered

a leather belt worthy of it
the memory of smoke

the Incident Response Pocket Guide
instructions admonitions tables for calculation

plastic slide rule
facts memorized facts misremembered forgotten

sling psychrometer and spare wick
small red bottle of sterilized water

backup windspeed meter
handheld scratched-up compass on a lanyard

lost pine forests of the Southeast
cry of the red-cockaded woodpecker

grubby spiral-bound notebook
for this log a pencil and pocket knife

Controlled Burn, Calloway Forest
    (after Chuang Tzu)

What more can be said about fire:
that it nibbles up the grass stalks,
and rips through the cane and tangle in the seep.

That is how the fire passes on.

All day I thought about nothing
but how much fire
to drop, or water, and how.

How fast to step through the slash, how far,
dipping the torch left or right.
Spot, spike, line, ring.

Whether to get out of the cab
and stamp out the flame sputtering
in the grassy track.

Wiregrass, scrub oak, longleaf
in grass stage, burned down; scorched
pinecones, ash and char.

This is how fire passes on.

Mill and Stone

The millstone set in a front yard
at the intersection of two roads
in Carrboro, North Carolina,

knows what we lost

in all that talk of stone,
stone against stone, which is best
for grinding, which can be got,
at what price;

what we lost

of the quarryman's work,
the miller's and the blacksmith's and the mason's,

and flour dust and stone dust
in the lungs, the hunger.

The dried corn, jittering and shushing
in the hopper, the crackling
quick-cut scissoring
grind between the millstones,

runner stone, bed stone, gossip and negotiations.

What is lost
of the stone's own language,
that comes in long slow waves,

stone years in the coming.

*

Water,
pouring

into the sluice and splashing
down the vanes
of the waterwheel,

hour after hour, as long
as there is water.

The clang and thunk of the water gate.

Old wood,
creaks, squeaks, scrapes,

the song of wood against wood
and wood against metal.

Metal,
a drone,
the round and round

of the spindle, the oiled gears, sliding
and whirring.

Water,
pouring.

*

This stone:

not one
but seventeen stones, cut
and pieced like a pieced quilt,

bound in a hoop of iron.

Burr stone, stone harp
for us to play on.

Oculus, eye
that draws the eye.

Little field,
with its lands, and what's left
of its sharp, straight furrows.

Mappa mundi,
in mildew and lichen,
in cavities and grain and inclusions,

its whole long story,
and the world
of our projections.

Bolin Creek at the Old Tripp Farm Road Crossing

The creek this morning lay
unmoored, drifting from the season

and its purpose, which is to roll seaward,

to do something more than soak
through small fissures in the bedrock.

Weeks of no rain and still

it gathers and channels a little water:
in its glossy

surface, trees unsettle.

It can do more than this. It knows
floods, a body like the human body

with habits and incidents

written into scars and healed bone—
that undercut bank and sandbar,

the wide meanders, rock rubble.

It knows us as stepping stones
and roadway, a mill in ruins,

the overgrown, washed-in millrace,

by the stones we throw in,
our selves in the likeness of stone.

Divination Stones

Most, I find under or alongside water:

lightly metamorphosed, residual
volcanics, conglomerates,

shards of old underground
and aboveground magma, lava, tuffs.

Here, now, in a wooden bowl:

a clutch of colors,
stones interrupted, unweathering

and uneroding, unless
I release them back into the water.

This small globe, this marble,

was a lump of damp red clay from the creek bank,
where the current

in flood, after days of rain, scrapes
its cutting edge.

I had to climb over a snarl

of roots and branches to reach that horizon.
They know: they tell

the past, and divine the future,

they can summon your lost
places, your lost people.

Fish Story

I dressed in the dark, inside out,
the neat, merrowed edges
of the T-shirt seams,
      all outward,
one label flagging the back neckline,
another tacked into the seam
at my side—
        like fins,
        vestigial.

It's hard enough
being human, so I was happy
being fish—

      though the real fish
in the real ocean
have it hard, too, what with
algae and oil spills,
      plastic, nets, fishing line.

But on and off
      all day
I slipped from the back deck
into the ocean
and the sounds of the world

became distant, the whoop-whoop
of sirens, muffled, the roar
and rumble of trucks, vans, cars
coming and going.

      My fish eyes
blurred and unfocused

on the images in the newspaper,

were good only
        under water,
for sliding through tall, flowing
kelp forests in the old field,

stands of crownbeard,
those flanged stems holding
the soft flop
        of their top leaves up to light,

for skirting brambles,
the coral-pink nuggets of unripe
blackberries.

        Out here,
it's all growing upward
from the inside out,

all leaf burst and incipient
        inflorescence:
the plant's trust
that everything will be okay,

or that living as if it will
is good enough.

Old House

It's still summer, and Gerardo Ruiz
and his son, Gerardo Ruiz,
have been at it all day, hammer and claw,
            prising off what can't be saved
            of the siding, under layers

of semisolid stain, under the wood grain
swollen with damp, and labyrinths
            drilled out by insects, plywood, particle board
blackened by decades of rainwater
                        seeping, streaking, down
            and drying, gone spongy, punky,
nails loosening, loose flashing.

They are, in this heat,
            ripping off the old boards
                        and letting them drop,
hoisting and clattering.

The house, we were so sure of it,
            inside and out,
                        its pipes and sump pump,
            water tank, HVAC, filters,
its wiring, its ducts and coils.

We abided with the insects and the birds,
the mice and roaches, the sugar ants
            running over the tiles and counters, they had
                        their pathways and lived off our largesse.
            We came to understandings.

The two Gerardos see a house

that is like ours,
                    that occupies
the same space and time, an overlay,
vulnerable and damaged,
           but still fixable, as we might see
our own bodies, or the earth.

After Moonset
         —for Sarah

There were no stars, nothing
moved that I could see,
under and among the trees.
No birdcall, no chitter
of squirrels, no daylight noises.
The fireflies had already faded
and dropped back into the layers
of night down in the leaf litter.
There was no wind, no color,
except the broad black strokes
and stipple and splotch of branches
and leaves, and, beyond them,
in the place of light,
an inky wash of sky, just visible,
just here and there, more
guessed than seen.

What there was, was the sound
of tree crickets, only
the crickets: their long
trills and short repeated chirrups,
their call-and-response chorus
from the trees, high up there
to my left, to my right, in front, the trees
behind the house, the here-be come-ye
of crickets, in a citadel of trees,
the males scraping wing on wing,
and the females, like me, drawn
to their call, intently listening.
They had their purposes, and I mine,
but it seemed they were saying

the Earth lives, it generates, it is wise,
it has its cycles, its day and night.
Trust it. And all around us
the many small sleeping
creatures of the woods
dreaming of woods everlasting.

Back in the Backyard

There was forest before this forest:
tree ferns
unnamed
extinct
conifers and angiosperms.

The cracked
rock and earth
are what's left of it.

Wind
in the crowns

and the puddling
shifting
shadows endless
iterations of its story.

Under the ghost
trees
I am

under pignut hickory
and oaks
among
loblolly saplings
storm litter
leaf upon leaf:

in the underworld
understory.

Human small
and strange
an emissary of sorts
or witness.

Can these lines
reach so far?
They are rooted
in this present.

Here's my dog.
Here's my wheelbarrow.

The Summer House at Banner Elk

All the runoff from this side of the mountain
trickles through a culvert running

under the house, its concrete-block pillars,
water pipes, wires, spigots, switches,

a woodpile, a trashcan, various meters,
and out through the yard of yellow birch and mosses,

downslope to the creek, to the Watauga River,
the Holston, the Tennessee, the Mississippi,

taking the shortest course—not
as a bird flies, but as water, colored

by everything it runs through: strata
still being laid down, or already abandoned.

You hear it day and night,
you sleep to the sound of it:

the child's toy buried under leaves,
a rusted grill, forest litter,

rock and sediment. Traces
of fire, and scrapers, arrow points.

If you follow the water, and the names,
you'll find the sorrow.

I Heard Rain

It falls,
        gathers, scatters,
        falls for miles, windswept

and slant, not new
        or simple, even now and when
        it falls into our lives

        (braid, unbraid,
        loose and fraying),

a weave of water,
        all rains past
        and future,

and somewhere, halfway through
        the night, a car
        stalls in a wash,

someone has placed a bucket
        to catch water dripping from a ceiling,
        rags along a sill

        (roof needs another patch,
        window needs caulking).

Child, are you home?
        Friend, did you find shelter?
        May the sump pump hold,

may the rooms
        not fill with groundwater,
        oil, sewage, bad dreams.

Husband, which letters,
        which photographs,
        will be the last we abandon?

October

Our road has become a boneyard
for children—

skulls, skeletons
litter the verges,

stick out of the red clay, or lie
in untidy heaps.

The road has become a funeral
of all the ones we lost.

R.I.P.,
dear or not, the coffins, the black plumes,

the procession of ravens and pumpkin heads—
a masque of children

and parents trailing
their own famished ghosts and hobgoblins.
Every year, the same tricks.
Caw, caw.

I Dreamt about the Dog

He limped along the margin
of the field in that skewed
scrawling walk of his,

his whole life telling in the knobbly bones
along his spine and rump.

Then broke into a run, bolted,
and I did not have to call him—
because he was gone,

as the tall grass has gone
to seed among the cedar
and loblolly.

To deer scat, old ball, the urine
of other dogs that forage here—
scents he knew,

the *fetch* and *come*
he knew before he knew our language.

When I Came to Myself Again

it was as grass
a common fescue but the soil
was not hardpan clay my roots
tingled crept down
pushed down
threaded through
the tiny voids
and hollows in the earth
life was good
there was water down there
leached minerals
and the bones and cartilege of our ancestors
    Whatever grew
above ground in the light
my roots could bear
could withstand the wind
and any weather
and they were not lonely
a million creatures
sheltered there among them
the fungi the one-celled travelers
they too moving in webs
the littlest thready worms all
talking to one another
in languages I did not understand
but being grass could hear
the buzz
the scrape and rub-against
the slip-stroke of their voices.
    So I reached up: sheath, shoot and stem and blade
into that exuberance
of beebait clover switchgrass plantain

robins pecking and jabbing
at earthworms cutworms
between my stems
    All through the grand parade of summer
I was dreaming small flowers
seeds
pipes and whistles
finches in the broomsedge
and treeleaves waving
even in the squalls my green
all whipped around
and slapped by thunder
crack lightning
my roots held
    Even when the mower ground
up and down the field
and cut me down
they held

Zap

was a shamble of a man:
his hair a wild upstart frizz, and his eyes
evasive. He had been struck
twice by lightning, and maybe
that was why he sat
panting and white-faced
under a tree and waited
while the rest of us kept working,
chopping and dragging brush
into piles for burning.
He liked the nickname, Zap,
his claim to fame,
his story—he'd survived,
he'd met, and dodged, his maker,
500 megajoules of god
coursing down his body
into earth. But I don't think
that was what he was feeling,
right then, in the shade.
The summer sorts us:
who can and can't
work all day in the field
and not be heat-struck, who
does and does not thrill
at the late-day summer storms
with all their drama
and chill downdrafts, the first
prickle of rain.
He knew lightning
is only looking
for the earth, and doesn't care
how it gets there or what

burns up, as long as it hits ground:
zig-zag and split: to this
particle, to that, down
cloud, tree, cliff, out of the blue,
a woman struck
dead on a bald mountain, a man
knocked down in a brush-infested field.

Speak Forest

Why so still, they ask,
why so heavy on the crisp needles
your crush-grass, moss-wheezy, flopsy limbs?
You sad?
Your roots not fingering down
into the soil and playing
with stones and small tunnels,
voles,
beetle shells?
Not sifting the crumbled leaves?
You clomp.
We is what was planted or what sprouted,
willy-nilly,
in a thin topsoil.
Blown about, swept off, leached soil, ploughed
by mule and tractor, shattered.
We rises
and looks down from our branches
to you on the leggy grass.
We flies
in dirt that's good enough already
and each year better, all duff, mould-leaf, caked pollen.
We knows
otherwise.
We gives way, takes advantage,
climbs up and over gravel and spoil heaps,
we is briars and creeper.
Water runs through we culverts,
we climbs up the eyes of wire-mesh fences
and trickles down.
We rots, we stumps and stump-holes,
we years of loblolly needles

drip and drape and shiver and skitter.
We trunks spiraled by vines, we vines.
Say, you come be post oak saplings and
yearlings, young cedars with us,
purple us foxgloves behind this split-rail fence.

Dendrology

The jitterbugging leaves
in the crown,

the leaf that falls
and drifts into the current—

how long do you need
to see a tree,

the distance it travels
beyond root and seeds,

all the before and after?
An ironwood, for example,

on the washed-out bank of Bolin Creek,
its spindly, irregular branches

and few leaves:
hop hornbeam, river tree,

tool wood, hubs and handles,
wood like the thin ropy arms,

of a carpenter, sleeves rolled up,
the one who called it

the prettiest wood he'd ever used,
and maybe the biggest

sonofabitch to work.

The tree lays down a long shadow:

once you step in,
there's no leaving it.

Field as Auditorium

What sound does a message make
as it loses itself in the ether
glissando diminuendo

What is the sound of my lost language
I hear a lilt and dive, music only

yr hen iaith fy mamau
a few passwords clicking from the keys

If I had said the things I wish now
that I had said, what would have been
the tone of her voice in answer

What did her smile sound like
I don't remember, she is so quiet

in her photograph, black and white, gazing off
What is the sound of a leaf falling
what kind of ear could hear it
as it shivers the air and slides down the wind
tremulo and thrum, pick-pick

the same as the grass growing but in reverse
What was the last call
of the last ivory-billed woodpecker

over the ordinary check-check twitter shrill peep
at dusk the end of November

In a Hard Year, Winter

Meanwhile, branches
drop, felled by wind
and rot.
Branches
crash into branches
break and
splinter.
I can guess
which ones will be
next,
by the white
mold on their black bark,

the frills of yellow fungus
on the boughs,
scales and
smudges of lichen.

Friends move
west or north,
first a cousin, then a sister
dies,
and all you can do
is write a note of sorrow.

The future is camouflage,
green and buff and grey,

waiting for you to step in,
to slide it up over your legs

and button up,
now your arms,
your hands, wiggling.

It fits, like bark
fits its tree,

like a dying body
fits the space it lies in.

Kindling

The trees in our backyard
slough off
bark, twigs, deadwood, leaves.

In time, the whole
old hickory and oak forest
with its buds and cankers,

burls, callouses, and scars
will end up here,
where I am, zigzagging

down the slope, scavenging
sticks and small branches
for a fire: the just fallen,

the not sodden or punky,
not mildewed,
or frilled or scaled with lichen,

before the beetles and woodlice
get their mandibles into it
and chew it up.

I have lost the sight
of one eye, and hearing—
lost, I say, as if I have been

careless or forgetful,
or could maybe find them
among the rocks and dead leaves.

I'll invent a ceremony
of twigs and matches
for their funeral.

Snow Loads in a Changing Climate: New Risks
    —Article by U. Strasser, Nat. Hazards Earth Syst.
    Sci., 8, 1–8

The snow let loose
in all its languages, its vulgar

native tongues,
curses and imprecations.

I transliterate, I compose:
whoosh, shhhh-ch-ch, thump,

and other, whiskery sounds
this side of hearing.

Why did the snow just slide off the roof,
just then, in the middle of the afternoon,

the shed roof, and slump, in a long
ridge of slush and icicles?

It seemed an omen, an echo
of icebergs cracking up and drifting,

of glaciers retreating, but it was just
a local thaw, and seasonal.

I arrived, I saw it, I thought
post hoc ergo propter hoc,

it slid because I was there,
with nothing else to do,

full of inchoate questions and no answers,
which then found shape and sound.

No, it was the air, the sun,
the pitch and aspect

and slick metal surface
of the roof, which until then slept

under its blanket and dreamt of sines
and cosines, calculations sublimated.

There was a silence then, as at the end
of a song, before the audience

comes back to itself,
and the earth, to its cataclysms.

Loose Ends

Between growing seasons, a flower
unravels, . . . forgets itself—

thinks,
as a flower thinks . . .

there was a color, or two, . . . light
floated upward and behind, . . . sky

wavered and fell, . . . roots
lost their footing . . .

decomposed
and recomposed, recollect—

something
to do with petals and stem, maybe also . . .
air—
it will come together

and begin again, though not
by itself

and not all at once . . .
when the days grow longer—

a filament here and there, . . . runners . . .
the stitchwork of generations

By the Almanac

it is time to plant

trees, if you have the heart for it:
bare-rooted plugs

dug up, their native soil still clinging to them,
or grown from seed or grafted, in potting mix,
seedlings, saplings, balled and burlapped,

but anyway dormant
and ready for planting, in cold soil,
to give them time—
and to give them space, the hole
must be twice the size of the root mass.

And not any soil, anywhere,
but crumbly damp till, and if all you have
is heavy clods of piedmont clay streaked with sand
dig it, use a shovel, planting blade, or hoedad blade,
stone pick, whatever, fork it and double fork,
break up and disperse and mix it up,
add compost and water.
This is called amending.

You want a dreamsoil, seedbed of nostalgia,
so the winter rain will wash it down
and fill the little air pockets
round the tender roots and hair roots,
settle the disturbed
soil around them,
and even so they may fail,
may already be dead.

The earth is tilted,
wobbling
into solstice, our part of the planet
leaning into the long nights and the intermittent familiar
waves of cold, frost, rain.

Chill and damp the old leaves.
Time too for raking, time to haul
twigs and leaves down into the woods
and give them back,
as root cover, shelter
for the smallest of earth's creatures,
those that nibble and gnaw and kill:
the myriad bacteria, fungi,
that make for scab and canker and rust and blight,
all equally thriving in this world.
And though the deer may nibble off the leaves
and rub branch and trunk bare
and the moths and caterpillars feed
and the spring rain fail,
it is the time for planting.
Though the planet is tilted
to disaster for us humans, currents
veering or fading, wind, flood, fire,
the days of judgment upon us, the year
and our years here ending,
it is time for planting

The Old Field, an Invocation

—*Cynefin* (Welsh): habitat, home place,
accustomed path

Few people come at this season, deer sometimes, but the
path down to the branch and along the creek is tamped
down to bare soil.

Cardinals in the thickets, an insistent wren.

On either side, it's a muddle of dead stiltgrass, autumn
olive, privet, arrowhead. The brown stalks of last year's
crownbeard, with its winged stems, its small seed crowns,
picked clean by the finches.

*Finches, sparrows. Their wing beats. The click and rustle of
their foraging and landings.*

Leaning canes, half of them dead. And native trees: young
evergreen cedars and pine, cork elm, deciduous
hardwoods—good deer cover.

Some of you I can summon by name: your common,
English names, my familiars. Hey, young tulip poplars;
hey, sweet gum; and you, red maples, oak saplings. My
footsteps send shivers along the ground and up your stems.

Another flurry of sparrows.

In your bodies, in your roots and branches, the voices and
racket of long-gone tree-fellers and farmers.

Pipe-pipe, chitter of cardinals.

In the bodies of insects, the beetles and woodlice in the stumps and rotted trunks of fallen trees. Eggs and larvae. In long narrow burrows under the older creekside trees, with the hibernating cicadas.

A squabble of crows.

We are all present now, all field-becoming-forest. Crows overhead, a whirling wheeling bevy of turkey vultures

Cardinals in the thickets, an insistent wren.

The Wilderness

between the concrete
sidewalk
and the concrete curb,
self-sown,
scaled down
to this narrow, parched
strip of earth,

is spreading,
as best it can;
seeding, dying back
to leaf and root crumble,
blown dust.

The air down at their level
is filthy
with black carbon, oxides, hydrocarbons,
gas and particles,

but the mosses,
the thin-bladed fescue gone
to seed, a radiance of grasses,
spillovers
of cloverleaf, broad-leaved
rosettes of plantain,
the sharp-toothed
dandelion,
the tiny yellow five-petaled
flowers and small
trifoliate leaves of wood sorrel,
clustered flutes
of white clover—

life could begin again
from such as these.

NOTES

Land considers the Martin Luther King Jr Park, Carrboro, Orange County, North Carolina.

The Field Index

Acrostic: Med. Lat. *acrostichis*, from Gk. *akrostikhi*s, from *akro*s "at the end, outermost" (from PIE root *ak- "be sharp, rise (out) to a point, pierce") + *stikhos* "line of verse," literally "row, line," from PIE root *steigh-* "to stride, step, rise" [Online Etymological Dictionary]. The Christmas fern's botanical name is *Plystichum acrostichoides* (Michaux) Schott.

André Michaux (1746–1802), French botanist, author of *Flora Boreali-Americana* (1803; "The Flora of North America"), made at least five visits to North Carolina.

Loblolly: *Pinus taeda*, From Wikipedia: The word "loblolly" is a combination of "lob," referring to thick, heavy bubbling of cooking porridge, and "lolly", an old British dialect word for broth, soup, or any other food boiled in a pot. In the southern United States, the word is used to mean "a mudhole; a mire," a sense derived from an allusion to the consistency of porridge. The pine is generally found in lowlands and swampy areas.

Manual of the Vascular Flora of the Carolinas, by Albert E. Radford, Harry E. Ahles, and C. Ritchie Bell (Chapel Hill: University of North Carolina Press, 1968). Commonly known as Radford.

Pleiades, Gk., perhaps literally "constellation of doves" from a shortened form of *peleiades*, plural of *peleias* "dove" (from PIE root *pel-* "dark-colored, gray") [Online Etymological Dictionary].

This Creek and *Before This the Occaneechi*. The Tutelo-Saponi words are used by permission of Native and Indigenous elders of Orange County, North Carolina. This area is part of the ancestral homeland of the Occaneechi Band of the Saponi Nation. Words and phrases of their language, one of the Souian family of languages, have been passed down by native speakers and by early visitors to the area. The terms I cite are borrowed from "A Grammar Sketch of Tutelo-Saponi," MA thesis by Robert Corey. Bolin Creek, named for an eighteenth-century colonial landowner, runs south-southeast through Orange County, joining other creeks that drain down into the Cape Fear River and out to sea.

Englynion for Fireflies and *Englynion for Moss*. Each stanza is an approximation of an englyn penfyr: a "short-ended englyn."

The poems about fire draw on my experience working with The Nature Conservancy on controlled burns in the Sandhills and coastal plain swamps of North Carolina.

Mill and Stone and *Loose Ends* were inspired by fabric art pieces by Lyric Montgomery Kinard

Field as Auditorium. The line in italics adapts a line from the Welsh national anthem. The original reads *yr hen wlad fy nhadau* (the old country of my fathers), here changed to *yr hen iaith fy mamau* (the old language of my mothers).

By the Almanac is in the form of a Fibonacci sequence.

ACKNOWLEDGMENTS

I'm grateful to Nery Levy for allowing me to use her artwork, *Dairyland Road Triptych,* for the cover. The image is of farmland in Orange County, North Carolina.

Thank you, too, to Barbara Ellertson, Lyric Montgomery Kinard, and all my companions and teachers.

The following poems have appeared in print or online publications, sometimes in earlier, slightly different versions.

"A Creek Too Small," *Tar River Poetry*

"Back in Backyard," "Controlled Burn Calloway," *Canary*

"Before This, the Occaneechi," *Panoply*

"Bolin Creek the Names," "By the Almanac," "Summer House at Banner Elk," *Poets for Science*, natureofourtimes.poetsforscience. org

"Dendrology," "Land," "The Wilderness," *Triggerfish Critical Review*

"Divination Stones," *Crosswinds Poetry Journal*

"Embroidered Field," "Passing," *New England Review*

"Englynion for Fireflies," *Seisma Magazine*

"*Erythronium americanum*," *Afield*, magazine of The Nature Conservancy

"Field as Auditorium," *Triggerfish*

"Honeysuckle," *Crosswinds Poetry Journal*

"In a Hard Year Winter," "Kindling," *Red Fez*

"In These Woods," "October," "Zap," *The Phare*

"Mill and Stone," *Stone, Water, Time*, exhibition catalog with art by Lyric Montgomery Kinard

"No Apples," Poetry in Public Spaces, NC Poetry Society

"Promised Land," *NC Literary Review*

"Speak Forest," *Indelible*

"Stitchwork," *Thrush*

"The Field Index," "Old House," *Terrain*

"*Verbesina occidentalis*," *Asheville Poetry Review*

"We Woods," *Verse & Image*

ABOUT THE AUTHOR

Maura High lives in North Carolina. Most of her poems concern this land and its inhabitants, human and other. She has won awards for individual poems and for her chapbooks, and is active in poetry groups and poetry events locally and nationally, as well as in her native Wales. Her work includes three chapbooks, *The Garden of Persuasions* (Jacar Press), *Stone, Water, Time* (Lyric Art Publishing), and *The Field Index* (Bolin Press), and poems in a number of print and online anthologies and magazines, among them *The New England Review, Southern Review, Tar River Poetry, Panoply, Terrain, Canary, Comstock Review,* and *The Phare.* For a fuller account of her work and interests, see www.maurahigh.com.